DISCOVER ♥ ♥ ♥
ORIENTAL SHORTHAIR CATS

Trudy Micco

The Cat Fanciers' Association, Inc.® (CFA™) was founded in 1906 as a not-for-profit association of member clubs and is the world's largest registry of pedigreed cats. CFA's mission is to preserve and promote the pedigreed breeds of cats and to enhance the well-being of ALL cats. CFA promotes education, responsible cat ownership, and proper care to the owners of millions of cats worldwide. CFA and its affiliate clubs work nationally with local shelters, at a grassroots level, to help humanely control homeless and feral cat populations, and to encourage voluntary neutering/spaying of pet cats. To learn more about the Cat Fanciers' Association, the pedigreed breeds of cats, or to find the nearest CFA cat show, visit their Web site at www.cfa.org.

Enslow Elementary, an imprint of Enslow Publishers, Inc.

Enslow Elementary® is a registered trademark of Enslow Publishers, Inc.

Library of Congress Cataloging-in-Publication Data

Micco, Trudy.
  Discover oriental shorthair cats / Trudy Micco.
    p. cm. — (Discover cats with the cat fanciers' association)
  Includes bibliographical references and index.
  Summary: "Early readers will learn how to care for an Oriental shorthair cat, including breed-specific traits and needs"—Provided by publisher.
  ISBN 978-0-7660-3853-0
  1. Oriental shorthair cat—Juvenile literature. I. Title.
SF449.O73M53 2012
636.8'2—dc22
                                    2011005898

Future editions:
Paperback ISBN 978-1-4644-0115-2
ePUB ISBN 978-1-4645-1022-9
PDF ISBN 978-1-4646-1022-6
Printed in China
012012 Leo Paper Group, Heshan City, Guangdong, China
10 9 8 7 6 5 4 3 2 1

To Our Readers: We have done our best to make sure all Internet Addresses in this book were active and appropriate when we went to press. However, the author and the publisher have no control over and assume no liability for the material available on those Internet sites or on other Web sites they may link to. Any comments or suggestions can be sent by e-mail to comments@enslow.com or to the address on the back cover.

Every effort has been made to locate all copyright holders of material used in this book. If any errors or omissions have occurred, corrections will be made in future editions of this book.

Photo Credits: Anja Hild/Photos.com, p. 23; AP Images/Frank Franklin II, p. 9; © blickwinkel/Alamy, p. 14; © Eugene Blackman, p. 17; Mark Herreid/Photos.com, p. 15; © Matthijs Rouw, p. 19; Mikael Hjerpe/Photos.com, p. 3 (left); Remi Turk, p. 13; Shutterstock.com, pp. 1, 3 (right), 6, 8, 11, 18, 22; © Tierfotoagentur/Alamy, p. 10; © Top-Pet-Pics/Alamy, p. 5.

Cover Photo: Shutterstock.com (gray cat).

Enslow Elementary
an imprint of
Enslow Publishers, Inc.
40 Industrial Road
Box 398
Berkeley Heights, NJ 07922
USA
http://www.enslow.com

CONTENTS

IS AN ORIENTAL SHORTHAIR RIGHT FOR YOU?

Oriental shorthair cats are very friendly. They like to be in the middle of anything you are doing. They also love to snuggle in your lap.

Cats go to the bathroom inside a litter box. You should clean the litter every day. Also, empty the box and wash it once a week.

Oriental shorthairs have smooth coats and big ears.

Kittens are cute and full of energy! Can you keep up?

A CAT OR KITTEN?

Most people like kittens. But kittens can be harder to care for than adult cats. They need more attention.

Older cats can be friendlier than kittens at first. Kittens need to get used to being away from their brothers and sisters. Is a kitten or an older cat better for your family?

LOVING YOUR ORIENTAL SHORTHAIR

Oriental shorthairs are very **loyal**. They will play with you and may follow you around. They can learn to come when you call them. You can also teach them how to play fetch.

Oriental shorthairs have a lot of love to share!

Cats practice their hunting skills with their toys.

EXERCISE

Oriental shorthairs like to climb. Make sure you have safe places for your cat to climb, like a **cat tree**. Also get special cat toys for your cat to play with.

Climbing and playing are exercise for cats. They need to exercise to stay healthy.

a cat tree

FEEDING YOUR ORIENTAL SHORTHAIR

There is wet food and dry food made just for cats. Feed and give your cat fresh water every day. A **veterinarian (vet)**, a doctor for animals, can tell you what kind of food and how much to feed your cat.

Remember to clean your cat's food and water bowls. Dirty bowls can make her sick.

You need special clippers to trim your cat's claws.

GROOMING

Oriental shorthairs have short hair. They can be brushed once or twice a week.

Cats scratch on a special post to keep their claws sharp. You can clip their claws once a month. A vet can show you how.

a pet brush

WHAT YOU SHOULD KNOW

Before you bring your new cat home, be sure your home is safe. Some plants are bad for cats.

Cats should not be allowed outside. Cars, mean people, and other animals can hurt them. Cats should stay indoors to stay safe and sound.

Cats enjoy looking out the window when they are indoors.

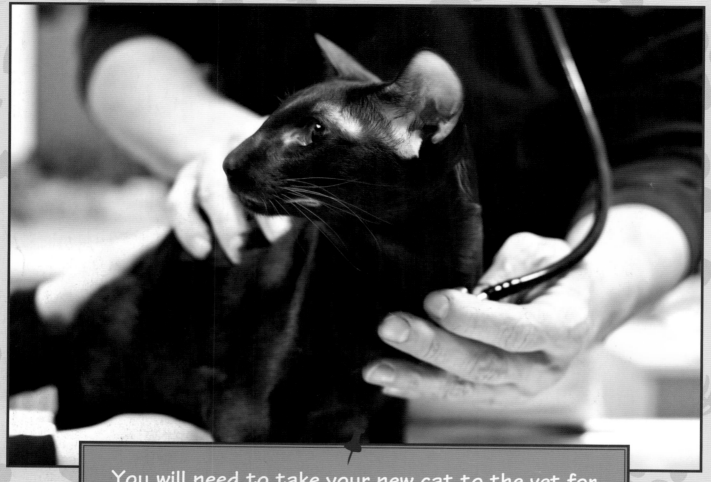

You will need to take your new cat to the vet for a checkup. He will need shots, called vaccinations, and yearly checkups to keep him healthy. If you think your cat may be sick or hurt, call your vet.

A GOOD FRIEND

Your Oriental shorthair will be a good friend to you for many years. Play with him, feed him, and take good care of him.

NOTE TO PARENTS

You can adopt your cat from a reputable breeder or from a rescue group that specializes in a specific breed. Spaying/neutering your cat prior to six months of age is advised. Neutering and spaying will prevent behavioral problems and many life-threatening diseases and help prevent overpopulation.

To keep your cat safe, keep him indoors. It is also a good idea to microchip your cat, in case he gets lost. A vet will implant a microchip under the skin that contains your contact information, which can then be scanned at a vet's office or animal shelter. Some towns require licenses for cats, so be sure to check with your town clerk. Also, check your home for potential dangers. Some plants and foods are toxic to cats. String can be very dangerous too. Cats like to play with it and sometimes they will eat it, which can cause them to get very sick and require surgery to remove. Ask your vet or visit www.cfa.org for a full list of concerns and for cat-proofing ideas.

Some things you will need before bringing your new cat home:

- **litter box** (Veterinarians recommend more than one in different places in the house.)
- **litter** (There are many brand choices.)
- **water and food bowls** (Use stainless steel, glass, crock, or other nonplastic material.)
- **cat food** (A reputable breeder will recommend a good quality food and how much to feed your cat, or ask your vet. The better quality the food, the healthier the cat, which means fewer trips to the vet's office.)
- **cat bed** (Select something the cat can snuggle into.)
- **special cat toys** (Select safe toys that do not have small parts or string that could come off and injure your cat.)
- **grooming brushes**
- **cat nail clipper** (or a human toenail clipper)
- **scratching posts** (There should be a few in different easily accessible locations in the house to keep the cat from damaging furniture.)
- **carrier** (Make sure your cat can stand up and move around in the carrier as an adult.)

cat tree—A tall thing cats can climb and play on.

litter box—A special box where cats go to the bathroom.

loyal—Always true to a friend.

vaccination—A shot that cats need to stay healthy.

veterinarian (vet)—A doctor for animals.

Books

Hengel, Katherine. *Outgoing Oriental Shorthairs.* Edina, Minn.: ABDO Pub., 2011.

Mattern, Joanne. *Oriental Cats.* Mankato, Minn.: Capstone Press, 2011.

Internet Addresses

The Cat Fanciers' Association: For Kids
<http://kids.cfa.org/>

ASPCA Kids
<http://www.aspca.org/aspcakids/

INDEX